The Amartsewe Playhouse Presents

What Has Food Got to Do with It, Anyway?

Ebsen William Amarteifio

Business Management BSc (Hons) DIP Journalism RMN

What Has Food Got to Do with It, Anyway?

(A Battle between Miss Positive and Miss Timid)

By E. W. Amarteifio

Illustrations by Sean Harper

Cover designs by Jason W. Amarteifio
BSc (Hons) Digital Media Development

authorHOUSE®

AuthorHouse™
1663 Liberty Drive
Bloomington, IN 47403
www.authorhouse.com
Phone: 1-800-839-8640

First published by AuthorHouse   12/06/2011

ISBN: 978-1-4567-8394-5 (sc)
ISBN: 978-1-4567-8395-2 (hc)
ISBN: 978-1-4567-8396-9 (ebk)

Printed in the United States of America

Any people depicted in stock imagery provided by Thinkstock are models, and such images are being used for illustrative purposes only.
Certain stock imagery © Thinkstock.

This book is printed on acid-free paper.

CONTENTS

Preface and Acknowledgements...ix

Introduction xvii

Scene One 1

Scene Two 11

Scene Three 17

Poetry Group...25

    1. Experience is the Best Teacher 25

    2. I Will Overcome...26

    3. No More Curves...28

    4. Sniff, Swallow, and be Sick...................................30

    5. Anorexia Nervosa..31

    6. Olivia Asks for Less..32

    7. I Want to be Like You...33

    8. Waiting for Happiness
        (The Proverbial No.12 Bus) 34

Soliloquy..37

Control..39

Steadfast..43

Weekend Leave At Home 45

Mary Jo..47

The Yoke, Fetters, and the Complexities
    of Anorexia Nervosa...51

Pauline and Baby Jewell...51

Justina and Baby Bassie 53

Competition and Rivalry
    in an Eating Disorder Unit......................................54

Close Observation...55

Boys? Not Boys! Yes Boys!!...57

Girl Power..57

Anorexia Nervosa and Boys...58

Polite and Cooperative...59

Understanding is Crucial 61

Body Image Problems...62

Narratives and Reflections 65

Broken Heart 65

First Year at University..66

Seclusion and Weight Loss...67

Copycat...68

Loss Of Weight...69

Low-Grade Jobs 71

False Allegation Ends Over Twenty Years
    of Dedicated Work..72

False Accusation 73

Other Thoughts and Observations 75

Family Ties..75

Our Mary...76

Lynchpin..77

Hospital Admission...77

Key Participant 78

Rivalry 79

Solidarity 79

Exercise 80

Who is Fat? 80

Who is Watching Whom? 82

Fathers 83

A Plan for Recovery 85

In Hospital 85

At Home 86

At Home—No Professional Support. 87

Who Wants to be in Hospital? 88

Some Facts and Figures 90

PREFACE AND ACKNOWLEDGEMENTS

My heart-felt thanks to a professor who is internationally known on the subject of eating disorders. After reading the play, he suggested that I could make a couple of points "more interesting". I duly obliged.

Sincere thanks to an eminent female consultant, also internationally renowned in the field of eating disorders. She had confidence in me and therefore kept me in her unit for thirteen years. About three years ago, in a family therapy setting, before the session started, she introduced me to the parents of the anorexic patient by saying, "This is Ebsen who has been in our unit for about ten years." It was an endorsement worthy of a thousand praises or an array of laurels.

Catherine Maxworthy? Yes, it was Catherine all right. She is an English girl with whom I worked for years at a general psychiatric ward. She became a team leader at the eating disorders ward and invited, "Come and work with me Ebsen." It was about thirteen years ago. I never looked back. Thank you, Catherine, wherever you are now.

Thank you also to all moral supporters, known and unknown.

There have been countless fond and interesting memories in the Eating Disorder Unit. It was a pleasure being part of a dedicated, multidisciplinary team caring for anorexics. A great number of girls and of course only a handful of boys were treated. However, I will mention only one girl whose name I have changed to Mari.

Having been on the ward only two days, she told me on the third night during medication that she would like to meet my children and "make friends with them".

"But they are a bit older than you," I stated.

"Never mind. I will be their baby sister," she retorted with a cheeky smile, which later became familiar to everybody.

Stunned by this unexpected approval, I could only agree,

"All right, then."

It is a shame she did not enjoy the luck of a chance meeting with them in either the Croydon or the Bluewater shopping centre. I could not arrange a meeting in the hospital for obvious reasons.

So what did all these people mentioned above see in me? Probably it is my Christian (Methodist) upbringing. If that is so, then I have Grandma Beatrice Nunoo of blessed memory to thank. She was a leading Methodist class leader of her day. My late father, George Agoe Amarteifio, was a pharmacist and a soloist of the main Methodist Church in Accra. My mother, Elizabeth Nunoo, is a staunch Methodist who still reads the Bible and quotes from it.

I am indebted to my wife, Susie, and my children, Wilma and Jason, for their patience and unflinching support. My sincere gratitude to all my brothers and sisters, for their moral support, especially my senior brother, Joseph Guy Amarteifio, a retired lecturer at Cape Coast University, Ghana. He was my mentor until I left home at twenty-three-years of age for England.

Many people have had a positive influence on me. My aunt, Comfort Sacker (Nee Nunoo), a teacher of blessed memory, influenced me from my infancy.

Special thanks to all my stepmothers, especially Madam Martha Naa Ami Nelson. Over forty years ago when I could not even afford a jacket without owing my mother the entire amount, Madam Nelson told me that she was sure that I would be one of the siblings to help the rest in the big family.

'Well, Auntie Naa Ami, I do not know what you saw in me. I have not done enough for the big family. I however hope that this project, which is my serious attempt to establish myself as a writer, will inspire the battalion of younger brothers, sisters, nephews, nieces, and others to aim for the next hurdle in their chosen fields. I know we have in the family two young university lecturers and others who have finished their university degrees and have already made their marks in their chosen professions. A host of others are striving to emulate what their seniors have achieved. There are also artisans making their mark in their chosen fields.

Aunt Naa Ami, if we had a road sweeper in the big family, I hope he or she would be inspired not only to be the best road sweeper at Korle Gonno or in a village at Kwabenya, but also to move on to become one of the best sweepers (if not the best) in the capital city of Accra.

If the publication of this book inspires anybody in the family to strive for the next hurdle, then the confidence you invested in me decades ago is about to yield fruits.

So as always young brothers, sisters, nephews and nieces, I know I am getting on a bit these days, but my passion and obsession over your academic and professional progress have not diminished even one pesewa. We want more directors, bank managers, and barristers.

Other relatives who have had positive influence on me are Cousin Edward Mensah, Chartered Insurance Practitioner and executive chairman of Edward Mensah, Wood & Associates Ltd., Accra, Ghana, and Uncle C.O.Tettey, who qualified as an engineer in Europe before returning to Ghana. His presence in the family house put my dreams in the overdrive slot.

I am also indebted to family friends Papa Lokko, Richard Amartei Amarh, and Mr and Mrs Sackey, both of blessed memory.

Lest I forget (how could I?), a special friend and a "brother"—Charles Amartey Aryiku, also from the Amartsewe Clan. He provided the required stimulus and academic challenge at secondary school. He is now living in Spain and is married to a lovely Spanish lady—Merche. They are blessed with two adult male children. Charles and I were both ardent supporters of Accra Great Olympics Football Team, formed in 1954 with my father as a founding member.

Another very good friend is Desmond Cornelius Dowuona. We were both teachers at The Radiant Way Preparatory School in Accra. We arrived in England on the same day in 1972 by British Caledonian Airlines. In the early years, during the bitter winter months, we moaned a lot as the cold weather permeated our African bones. We now look back with fond memories. Ike Ennin is another very good friend of exemplary character who also helped make the initial harsh winters a bit more bearable.

I cannot complete this preface without mentioning an interesting episode during my first year in a NHS adolescent unit with some anorexics. The consultant of the unit was one Dr Steinberg, who was well respected and progressive in his ideas.

One night, I was administering medication when I heard somebody screaming from the ward downstairs. I will call the girl who was screaming Bek.

When I listened intently, I heard, "You murderers! You cannot put this poison in my body! Murder! Murder! Murder! *Help!* Somebody help me from these vile nurses."

In a bid to calm Bek down, a female nurse brought her upstairs for a walk. She was still screaming, but not as loudly, as they emerged at the top of the stairs.

When they saw me, the nurse said, "Say hello to Ebsen."

Bek was still crying but was reasonably calm and said, "Hello, Ebsen."

"Hello, Bek," I answered back. "Who were the people troubling you downstairs?"

"Murderers—evil people—they want to make me fat," she said with a sob.

"She refused to drink her hot chocolate," the nurse explained with her arm around Bek's waist.

"They want to make me fat," Bek said.

"Calm down, calm down," I said.

"She refuses to have any snack at all," the nurse said.

"But what about all these millions starving in Africa?" Bek questioned.

In response, I took an unopened airmail letter from my breast pocket, waved it in the direction of Bek, and said, "Look, Bek. My brothers sent me this letter. They said that the food is getting through."

"All right then," she said as she wiped her face and with some composure also put her arm around the nurse's waist.

As they were returning to their ward, the nurse looked back at me and gave a wink of approval.

It could also have meant "cross your fingers", since as the behaviour of an anorexic is concerned,. when you think you have made a breakthrough, that is when the battle starts anew. They suddenly realize that they have given away some control.

Anyway, I returned to the office and settled into a chair feeling proud of myself. I had hardly savoured ten minutes of my new achievement when I heard yet another scream.

"Murderers, murderers! You make me fat! Look at all these Africans starving!"

The next moment I heard my name being called out, "Ebsen, come and finish what you started."

"Oh, dear," I said under my breath.

It took another hour before Bek drank the hot chocolate.

INTRODUCTION

What Has Food Got To Do with It, Anyway? is a book (which includes a short play) about the illness anorexia nervosa. In the play, I focused on one girl to underscore the prevalent characteristics of people (mainly young women) suffering from this pernicious illness.

A principal characteristic of this disease is the constant struggle or battle going on in the mind of each girl to think and behave positively or think like an anorexic and behave negatively. The more negative they are in behaviour, the more they are ensnared by this illness.

The struggle between positive and negative emotions is very evident when patients are in hospital. Needless to stress, the majority of sufferers do better in hospitals or institutions (away from loved ones) where treatment programmes are implemented and followed properly.

Another example is how some sufferers—patients—use the illness as a tool or power to control family members or loved ones. Some constantly look depressed or unhappy and feel guilty if they ever look cheerful or enjoy themselves, however brief that enjoyment may be.

I have written eight poems, which appear in the book, to depict in different ways the effects of this pernicious illness, and at the same time, I offer pockets of encouragement for survival and full recovery:

1. Experience is the best teacher
2. I will overcome
3. No more curves
4. Sniff, swallow, and be sick
5. Anorexia nervosa
6. Olivia asks for less
7. I want to be like you
8. Waiting for happiness (the proverbial No. 12 bus)

In "I want to be like you", written through the eyes and imagination of a twelve-year-old girl, I wanted to highlight how the lifestyle and general behaviour of celebrities in the world of glamour could affect the lives of young people, especially girls. However, it is not the main reason why some girls become anorexic. Leading consultants maintain that the problem is complex.

In a typical year, there could be an average of twenty-four girls between the ages of twelve and seventeen admitted to the eating disorders unit and treated by the multidisciplinary team. Many patients would be well enough after some months of inpatient treatment to continue with their recovery at home in the care of the various community teams.

My background in the medical field is in general psychiatry as a nurse (RMN), but I have worked for thirteen years in the specialist field of eating disorders. It would be presumptuous of me to say that I am an expert in the field. However, what I know is that one can understand anorexics without necessarily agreeing with them.

Once a treatment programme is formulated—it includes diet, therapy, and in some cases medication—one should piously stick to its implementation and appraisal, when necessary. The typical anorexic will ceaselessly contrive in various ways to test the resolve of the multidisciplinary team. They do so by targeting individual team members. The more resolute a member is, the more he or she is hated by some anorexics. Patients eventually come to appreciate that dogged stance when they are recovering or fully recovered. They often say how capable and, above all, how professional and fair that member of the team is.

Decisions! Decisions!

SCENE ONE

[Music: classical or any soft music

08.00 hours: on the ward.

The long corridors on the ward are quiet. The night lights are still on. Most of the girls are in bed; a few are up but still in their rooms. The morning staff have already taken over the shift.

A peep through the office window reveals a calm morning. The trees in the garden are devoid of the snow drops that adorned them the previous week. A rare January sun appears to be breaking through behind the long line of deciduous trees that form the borders of the hospital's sprawling garden.

A thaw has allowed the lush, green blades of the grass to emerge again. Half a dozen squirrels are foraging for food. A large one chases a small type up one of the tall trees. It is difficult to say whether the squirrels are at play or the big one is herding the cheeky intruder out of his acquired territory. In the far corner of the garden, a black bird

1

has in its beak a big worm still quivering with life. A lone magpie, unruffled by two fluffy pigeons fighting over a tiny worm, takes centre stage.

A leisurely walk in this beautiful garden is tempting despite the cold, but the slush is still evident from a distance.

RAP! RAP! RAP!]

First Nurse: Wakey wakeeee! You sleeping beauties; it will soon be breakfast.

[Some of the girls respond immediately by coming out of their rooms and forming a short procession towards the office—first to use the office toilet and then be weighed.]

Second Nurse: Hey! Sleepy head, don't tell me you have already used the toilet. No water holding, dear.

First Patient: Yes! I have.

Second Nurse: That was quick. All right, jump on the scale.

[She walks gingerly towards the scale, but the nurse suddenly but gently restrains her by holding her arm.]

First Patient: What is the matter now?

Second Nurse: Wait a minute—let me look under this mop of West Country hair and see whether you are again hiding those big, heavy earrings. Are you Pat Butcher?

[The first patient immediately parts her hair on either side of her ears to reveal flat ear lobes without rings of any size or description: not even a string hanging from either.]

First Patient: Satisfied?

Second Nurse: Yes, darling. When it comes to you young girls, one cannot be too careful. Once beaten . . .

[She completes the saying with a sarcastic giggle.]

First Patient: Twice shy!

Second Nurse: At least you now know that I am as vigilant as ever. You need to earn your pass and other privileges by regaining real weight not by relying on any other thing to tip the scale in your favour.

[The two nurses in the office go through the process of weighing all the girls and recording (out of view) their respective weights.

They join two more nurses on duty in the communal area where other girls, changed and dressed up, are waiting. Breakfast in the dining room starts at 08.00 hours.

Enters our subject who is played by two girls, Miss Positive and Miss Timid.]

Miss Positive: Food is sustenance. It sustains health and growth. We cannot do without it.

[She says this under her breath. She stops briefly and starts to sing "Food glorious food, hot sausage and mustard . . ." Miss Timid appears restless and looking irritable. She screams . . .]

Miss Timid: *Stop it! Stop it! Stop it!* I cannot take anymore. All day yesterday, you could think of nothing but how good food is and all that. I've had enough. It is not fair.

[She shows her frustration, oblivious of who is present and listening. Is she hearing voices?]

Miss Positive: My dear Timid, let us face facts. Have we not been living a lie for a long time?

Miss Timid: Why do you say that?

Miss Positive: I mean . . .

Miss Timid: You mean what? Can't you explain what you mean?

Miss Positive: I mean, what has food got to do with it?

Miss Timid [*shouts angrily*]: What has food got to do with what ?!

Miss Positive: I mean this illness we have put on ourselves has nothing to do with food.

Miss Timid [*she seems out of breath as she shouts angrily*] It has! It has! It has!

Miss Positive: If it has, prove it then.

Miss Timid: Why do you keep on about this all the time? You are making me ill.

Miss Positive: No, I'm not making you ill. I want you to face facts. You have made us live a lie for far too long.

Miss Timid: What lie?

Miss Positive: We used to eat like everybody else did. We enjoyed all types of food. We did not fear any food.

Miss Timid: You mean we were making ourselves fat and bloated.

[*She seems to regain the initiative.*]

Miss Positive: We were not fat. Come off it.

Miss Timid: So what were we? Answer me.

Miss Positive: I can explain. Just please listen. You have had your way far too long. It has not helped us.

Miss Timid: So what is it then, clever one?

Miss Positive: So you pretend that you do not know or recollect. Didn't Mum and Dad put excessive pressure on us to work hard and emulate big sister's academic excellence? Food has nothing to do with it.

[Our subject runs to her room and sobs uncontrollably. Soon, the supervising nurse calls out.]

Supervising Nurse: Breakfast! Breakfast! Breakfast!

[The girl gently gets up, looks into the mirror, and wipes her tears. She walks out of her room towards the dining room.]

Miss Positive: Since you do not refute my explanation, from now on you have to listen to me for a change, if we want to get better and resume normal living.

[A brief silence ensues as if Miss Timid is pondering the truth.]

Miss Positive: From now on, we should say to ourselves we cannot change the past but learn from the experience. We should make maximum use of the present. We should not let the bitterness of the past cloud the present and leave us unprepared for the uncertain future.

[The scene changes to the dining room—our subject sits at the breakfast table and stares at her meal: a bowl of cereal, two pieces of

toast, and natural yoghurt. She bursts into tears as others are about to eat.]

Miss Positive: Pull yourself together and get on with it. How long are you going to inflict this pain on us? I for one will not take it anymore. Today is a new chapter in our life.

Supervising Nurse: Pull yourself together, young lady. You have to overcome this illness. The meal in front of you is nothing at all. A four-year old would finish it off before you pronounce the dreaded phrase "eating disorder".

[Our subject sits up, looks around the dining table, and finds that everybody is looking at her. She wipes her tears.]

Miss Positive: You see, they are all looking at us. Let us show them that today marks a different chapter in our life.

Miss Timid: Have we not been here before? We failed and failed each time, miserably.

Miss Positive: Yes we have, but today is different. I will dictate terms from now on.

[Our subject, with a bit of renewed confidence, finishes her breakfast without more tears.]

Supervising Nurse: Well done, my dear. It doesn't hurt at all does it? Learn to like and enjoy your food.

[09.00-10.00 hours. This is an hour of supervision and rest before the group activity. Our subject joins the rest in the communal area.]

Miss Timid: I don't know. I feel fat already. Why should they increase the cereal for goodness sake?

Miss Positive: Stop kidding yourself. If you feel fat, I don't.

Miss Timid: I wonder what it is for lunch today.

Miss Positive: Stop it! Stop it! For goodness sake! We have just finished one meal; why worry ourselves with the next one, which is not due for over three hours?

Miss Timid: If they left me alone to eat what I want and when I want to, I would not be preoccupied with food.

Miss Positive: This sounds reasonable, but you know that if we were left on our own you would starve us to death.

[There is silence, and Miss Timid does not respond.]

Miss Positive: We were close to death when we collapsed and were admitted into hospital. Remember?

[Our subject is sitting with others in the communal area, but she battles with herself, oblivious to all around her. She is given three pieces of mail—two cards from close friends from her college and a

letter from her big sister. She holds them in her hand for about thirty minutes without realizing it.]

Supervising Nurse: Young lady, as far as I know, you have been holding these letters all day. Are you not going to read them? Count yourself lucky. Not many girls get as many letters as you.

[Miss Timid is about to say "It is none of your bloody business," when Miss Positive prevails].

Miss Positive: Oh! Oh! I am sorry I will read them when I have enough time.

[A feeble, but plausible, excuse to stave off the unwanted attention of the supervising nurse and, of course, of the other girls in the communal area.]

Miss Timid: Do you have to give excuses all the time when people are being bloody inquisitive?

Miss Positive: I don't, but diplomacy has never been your forte, so leave things to me in future. Sometimes you are too flippant for my liking.

[The clock reads 09.55 hours. The group therapist appears.]

Therapist: Group activity in five minutes. Ladies, get ready. I will be waiting in the TV lounge.

A patient by the lounge window

SCENE TWO

[Music: classical or any soft music. *A spacious lounge with a TV centrally positioned by the wall opposite the entrance. A beautiful aquarium occupies one corner. Half a dozen colourful fish in their habitat of stones, shining pebbles, young green shoots, a stranded anchor stuck in clear white sand, and of course a lit fluorescent tube offer a captivating sight.*

Two sofas and a high table are strategically placed in this lounge. There are a number of soft cushions to give comfort.

A look through any of the windows reveals sections of the sprawling, beautiful garden.

The clock reads 10.00 by the time all the patients and the two attending nurses are seated. A banner reading "Thought for the Day" is pinned on the wall.]

Therapist: In the last few weeks, each of you made strenuous efforts to delve into the causes of your problems. You have to be true to yourselves. It is the only road to recovery.

Miss Timid: It is of no use.

Miss Positive: Shut up and leave matters to me. Others have delved into their past and successfully identified factors of their illnesses. We both know that they are better for it.

Miss Timid: I say it is a bloody waste of time. These nurses, therapists, doctors, and whatnots are here just for the money. Their ideas do not work in practice.

Miss Positive: Don't be flippant. Stop being stubborn and negative all the time.

Therapist: In the last few weeks, about four of you have been able to identify what gave rise to your illnesses. We shall continue to conduct general discussions here. I will continue to offer one-to-one private sessions to encourage each of you identify the reasons behind each illness and hopefully begin to find agreed-on and workable solutions.

[The therapist allows five minutes for the girls to sit quietly and reflect on what she has said so far.]

Therapist: I want the name of one volunteer before we read our "Thought for the Day" passage. After that, our special one-to-one sessions will now be known as "Reflections".

[Meanwhile, our subject appears restless and seems to be agonizing over what to do. Suddenly, she stands up.]

Miss Positive: I will stand up and read the poem I wrote for everybody to hear.

Miss Timid: No! You do no such thing. I told you not to write it. Please! Please! Don't read it.

Miss Positive: I will ignore your pathetic plea and read it.

Therapist: Splendid, read it now. I will still offer you one to one at 15.00 hours.

[Our subject brings out a folded paper. She adjusts her dress, gently caresses her hair, and looks nervously around as if she was soliciting encouragement from the rest of the girls. Some of the girls applaud politely while others smile to encourage her.]

Miss Positive: The title of my poem is called "My Secret".

Miss Timid: You are going to make a laughingstock of us.

Miss Positive: Will you please shut up?

Therapist: Come on dear—you can do it.

Miss Positive: "My Secret"

My big sister was studious.
She was a book worm.
A head for figures and words.
In short, Miss Clever Clogs.

In school, she wrote the best essays.
She was also tops in maths.
She never tired of learning.
She was the teachers' darling.

Mum and Dad were very proud.
They talked about her to friends.
Showed her off even to strangers.
Seemed forever singing her praises.

When she got her first-class degree,
I was suddenly no longer in her shadows.
Exposed I was to extreme parental pressure.
Pressure I could not bear.

I fell ill under the pressure.
I became depressed and isolated myself.
I ate only small portions of my meals.
Sometimes, I did not eat at all.

I lost weight and my parents became alarmed.
They started quarrelling often.
Blaming each other for my condition.
I never answered any of their questions.

Suddenly the pressure was off me.
I did not have to emulate my big
sister's academic excellence.
I stopped my studies and remained at home.

The more weight I lost, the more
I was pampered.
Have I found my secret weapon?
It certainly felt like it.
I would cherish it and use it to my advantage.

[Subject finishes reading her poem.]

Therapist: Well done! You are brave. This is a revealing account. Yet another example of how food or the rejection of it can be used to mask an entirely different problem. I hope those of you yet to volunteer will be encouraged by this frank account.

[The therapist and Miss Positive retire to their respective seats after the reading.]

SCENE THREE

[*Music: classical or any soft music.*

The lounge: a centre table with a vase of flowers on it. A comfortable chair at either side of the table. A few attractive framed pictures adorn the walls.

15.00 hours.
Time for one-to-one session with the therapists and our subject.]

Therapist: Welcome to this private session. I am glad you managed to read your poem.

Subject: I initially found it difficult to read my account. I am glad I did finally pluck up courage in front of everybody.

Therapist: I was pleased with your performance. I am sure many of the girls were impressed and encouraged. Well done!

Subject: Thank you.

[She feels very pleased with herself and appears to gain some confidence from this initial exchange.]

Therapist: Tell me, did you at anytime think that you were punishing your parents by starving yourself?

Subject: It felt like it, because after the sustained pressure they put me under, it seemed that I was beginning to fight back.

Therapist: By starving yourself and losing a lot of weight, were you not punishing yourself as well?

Subject: It did not occur to me that I was punishing myself. I just wanted them off my back. Once they relented, I knew I had found my weapon irrespective of the apparent harm I was causing myself.

Therapist: When did it stop being a weapon to ward off your parents and become a daily ritual or competition with yourself?

Subject: About six months ago.

Therapist: What happened or what did you do?

Subject: Having put my parents in their place, it seemed only natural to raise this thing—.

Therapist: What thing? Do you mean the illness?

Subject: I suppose so, but at that time I did not feel that it was an illness. I was fat and needed to lose weight. I had to take it to a higher level. Yes! It was like a competition to test my willpower and how far I could push myself.

Therapist: What changed, and may I ask, when did you realize that you had been gripped or ensnared by this illness?

Subject: Well, five months ago I collapsed and was admitted into hospital.

Therapist: Were you frightened?

Subject: Frightened? I was doubly petrified. I knew then that I had gone too far.

Therapist: What was your parents' reaction?

Subject: They were also petrified. I could see their ashen faces. My Dad appeared to have lost a couple of stones from his pot-belly overnight. Mum is naturally slim so there wasn't much change.

Therapist: How supportive were they when you were admitted into hospital?

Subject: Mum was very supportive, but I suppose I had her wrapped around my little finger and made her spoil me rotten. She gave in to all my whims.

Therapist: What about Dad?

Subject: He was a bit supportive initially. After some days, he became grumpy and most of the time inpatient. The more he got on my nerves, the more resolved I was. Sometimes, they disagreed and often had rows in my presence.

Therapist: What about big sister?

Subject: She was sometimes supportive and sometimes indifferent. I suppose if I had given her half a chance she would rather be discussing the latest book she had read than discuss calories and weight.

Therapist: Before you stopped college, did you feel different among your friends?

Subject: Not really. Many of us were in the same boat—starving ourselves senseless. One particular girl would starve herself and exercise for hours in the gym. She would then stuff her stomach with a lot of food only to dash to the toilet and be sick.

Therapist: That is bulimia. What do you reckon were the actual reasons behind some of your friends' poor eating habits?

Subject: On reflection, I can say that some dieted rigorously because of peer pressure, others because of exam worries, others like me felt family pressure, and some were simply not ready for the responsibilities of growing up.

Therapist: Were there some with relationship problems? I mean boyfriend problems.

Subject: I knew of one, but there could have been more.

Therapist: I see you are now making steady and encouraging progress in this unit. What plans have you got for the future?

Subject: I am determined to carry on with my progress by seeking appropriate help, go back to college, and finish my A levels.

Therapist: Then what?

Subject: I want to study fashion and design, a field I know I can excel in.

Therapist: Do your parents know of your future professional plans away from academic goals?

Subject: They now know, and I hope they do not make any attempt to dissuade me from my cherished goal. If they support me, then all will be well.

Therapist: If not?

Subject: Let us simply say that I would not brook any opposition from any quarter.

Therapist: You have been in this eating disorder unit for about four months. Are you clear in your mind the root cause of your illness?

Subject: I think it is obvious.

Therapist: Well, spell it out.

Subject: Of course, it is my parents' severe pressure on me to emulate my big sister's academic excellence, coupled with my inability to passionately convince them that I could not achieve that feat. Given the appropriate support, I would excel in fashion and design.

Therapist: What has food got to do with it?

Subject: I suppose it has nothing to do with it.

Therapist: Thank you!

Subject: My pleasure!

Patients at a poetry group

POETRY GROUP

[First patient reads]

1. EXPERIENCE IS THE BEST TEACHER

Experience is the best teacher.
Mother is the First Teacher.
The past is full of experiences, good and bad.
The good experiences offer fond memories, whereas the bad provoke
Regret
Anger
Frustration
Bitterness
Sadness
Restlessness
Agitation
Sometimes extreme pain.

The endearing events of the past should not hold us to ransom. Conversely, the negative past should not shackle our progress in life.

The fetters of pain, bitterness, and sadness should not disturb our attention for today or the present.

The burden of anger, regret, and agitation of yesterday should open our eyes for the unfolding events of today and the unknown tomorrow.

Our parents, trusted relations, and appointed officers should be our eyes, ears, and feet in the long, arduous, and often unpredictable walk of life. (We do not walk alone. We will never walk alone.)

They (parents, etc.) should be our navigators for the uncharted waters of tomorrow; else we shall be swamped by the avalanche of responsibilities and problems of growing up.

Be lifted by the good memories of yesteryear but be wise by the "negatives".

[Second patient reads]

2. I WILL OVERCOME

Why am I here?
There is nothing wrong with me.
My parents brought me here.
The nurses do not like me.

Hawkish devils at meal times
Ready to shovel the tiniest
Food crumb back into my mouth.
I hate them.

Whose body is it anyway?
It is mine, and there is nothing wrong with me.
It is so unfair.
They do not allow me to do anything.

They are always demanding.
They are always uncompromising.
Why should they be so cruel?
I am trapped. No freedom.

They tell me what to eat.
I cannot even go for a walk.
They always keep watching me.
I feel it is unfair.

These were my thoughts, observations, and experiences during the heady days when I thought that there was nothing wrong with me. Nobody could convince me. The nurses had conspired with my parents to make me fat. It was the only thing they were interested in.

I questioned.
I probed.
I pondered.
I wondered.

Why! Why!! Why!!!
I used to say to myself.

"It is not fair . . . not fair . . . not fair." I cried myself to sleep many a night.

Everybody seems to be nice to me now. Even the nurses, who I thought were very demanding, uncompromising, and sometimes evil, hug me and smile sweetly at me when I achieve a target.

I am not out of the woods yet, they tell me. However, I can see the light. I do not feel trapped anymore. I am determined that, with the continued work of the medical and nursing team and my parents' support, I will overcome this illness.

There will surely be hurdles on the way, but I will succeed as thousands and thousands of other girls have.

One day, not very, very long, I will look back on this period, regard it as just a "blip" in an already rich and fulfilling life with lots and lots and lots more to look forward to.

[Third patient reads]

3. NO MORE CURVES

I was proud of my curves,
For I had many admirers.
The attention was intoxicating,
The belief was overwhelming.

An old family friend he was,
A young innocent girl was I.
He abused me and shattered my trust.
I suddenly realized my naivety.

I felt dirty after the experience.
I washed and washed and washed.
Secretly I cried and cried and cried.
Everything was lost, so was my pride.

I blamed myself for the attraction.
I never thought of that reaction.
How would my parents react?
Is this part of growing up?

I feigned illness to avoid school.
I cut myself off from my family.
I ate little and lost weight.
Suddenly, I found the distraction.

But I carried the shame and the guilt,
That burden and regret not for young shoulders.
I finally confided in my mother,
And the long road to recovery began.

[Fourth patient reads]

4. SNIFF, SWALLOW, AND BE SICK

My mother was a professional cook,
Long before this era of celebrity chef.
I liked the smell of food:
But to eat was to believe.

At eighteen I went to college.
Delighted but missed mum's cooking.
"I will supply you with chicken
'n the other favourites," she promised.

My peers were as studious as I.
Fixed academic aspirations, so did I.
Wicked sense of humour, so did I.
Everything in common but my BMI.

I had to shed to be "pretty" like them.
What about mum's tasty meals?
I cried as I struggled to cope.
Suddenly I lost to look "pretty".

I started enjoying food again.
I sniffed the aroma of food.
I ate and swallowed any food.
Straight after, to the loo and be sick.

[The Therapist reads]

5. ANOREXIA NERVOSA

Anorexia nervosa, the snare to avoid.
A shackle to distort logic.
A net entrenched in concrete.
An enclosure to keep family away.

Such illness, a vice so powerful.
A pain so visible to all but her.
Jaws so wide and uncompromising.
Talons to tear away the human form.

Anorexia nervosa, a yoke to bear.
A burden too heavy for young shoulders.
A weight to retard any progress.
A blow to get her down.

Hurray! Considerable progress made.
Achieved through a mass of haze.
We can see but not out of the woods,
For the beast is complex and pernicious.

[The Therapist reads her second poem]

6. OLIVIA ASKS FOR LESS

Olivia had the features of a fashion model.
She longed to be in the fashion limelight.
Mum craved to have a model in fashion.
The fame, fortune, and adulation, the pull.

Olivia watched and adored the leading models.
She read about their captivating lifestyles.
She dressed and walked as they:
Mannerism and temperament in equal measure.

"The curves must go" to achieve parity with her heroines.
A consensus, carried but not a muffled protest from Mum.
An impressionable age is the period of absorption.
But a mature age is the realm of advice and caution.

Olivia restricted her food intake.
The target was achieved in no time.
Sadly, anorexia reared its form.
The snare of this pernicious illness clicked.

A long period of hospitalization and respite.
Recovery, frustratingly slow but encouraging.
Mother and daughter, lesson—painfully learnt.

[The youngest patient reads an essay]

7. I WANT TO BE LIKE YOU

My friends and I watched a beauty pageant at school two years ago when I was ten. The winner was a sixth former called Mary. All the girls thought that she had a pretty face. The boys said that she had a "wicked" body. I just wanted to be like her.

Last year, she lost some weight and became a fashion model. She appeared on TV, the glossy magazines, and in all the newspapers. She travelled to many exotic countries for photo shoots. She won the "Model of the Year" award. She became famous and rich. Everybody liked her. Every time I saw her, she appeared to be slimmer and prettier.

I put her enlarged picture in my bedroom. I also cut down on my food to look as pretty as she. I could look at her picture for hours.

This summer, she is returning to my school to be presented to all the children. I am in hospital where I should not be. There is nothing wrong with me. If I could only have the opportunity to say to her, "I want to be like you."

[A day-care patient reads]

8. WAITING FOR HAPPINESS (THE PROVERBIAL NO.12 BUS)

Waiting for happiness or relying on somebody for happiness is like waiting for the proverbial No. 12 bus.

The driver might have had a quarrel with the wife this morning. Even worse, he might have had a quarrel with the mother-in-law last night after returning from the pub. The bitterness lasts longer.

He could fall ill in the eleventh hour or injure his leg when entering the bus.

The bus could suddenly develop a mechanical fault.

All right, so the driver did not have a quarrel with the wife. The cantankerous mother-in-law did not pick up a fight with him. He was well and fighting fit this morning.

He successfully managed to start the bus.

What about the roads? Well! The mayor of London could decide (suddenly) to lead a long procession through the centre of town. Long delays and diversions would ensue.

A getaway robber's white transit van could smash into the front of the bus.

A police horse could suddenly gallop into the road causing pandemonium. Another delay.

British Gas could suddenly decide to dig the middle of the road for emergency repairs. Not to have been outdone, Thames Water would suddenly decide to come back, dig the road, and recover the local manager's all-important log book inadvertently buried underground.

If my No. 12 bus eventually arrives, it is likely there will be two more following. It would have taken so long that my frustration would have turned into a deep-seated depression. I do not think I would be able to enjoy the ride.

Do not be afraid to be happy or look happy. Do let your sense of fun and humour prevail; enjoy them in other people, in what you read in books, watch on TV, or what you hear on the radio.

Be happy even if it means just fleeting moments every hour of the day.

SOLILOQUY

Anorexia nervosa is a complex illness and, in many cases, has immense psychological undertones. The less anorexic patients eat, the more successful they feel. The thinner they get, the more attention and pampering they receive from some parents and loved ones.

Patients normally resist treatment, but the majority—thankfully—relent and accept treatment. National Health Service figures reveal that admission in the last ten years has doubled.

Nothing is assured; the multidisciplinary team of doctors, dieticians, nurses, and therapists (with sometimes the constructive contribution of some parents) has to be consistent and focused throughout.

Some anorexic patients may be withdrawn, quiet, depressed, and appear aloof, but given the slightest chance, they will exploit the weakest link to avoid or restrict food. They always test and push boundaries. Firmness and fairness are needed at all times.

Cheating, unfortunately, is synonymous with the behaviour of some anorexics. No matter how vigilant and observant a nurse is, anorexics will succeed in cheating now and then. Cheating at meals in the presence of other sufferers of anorexia has damaging consequences.

Firstly, it puts off those who are genuinely doing their best to beat this dreaded illness.

Secondly, it encourages those in denial to do the same and get away with it.

Thirdly, it is a bad example to set in the presence of sufferers who are in hospital for the first time. Finally, once somebody gets away with cheating at meals, that person is bound to continue with that practice to the annoyance of other patients. Recovery then becomes initially stifled while the long-term prospect becomes frustratingly doubtful.

An apple or any piece of snack that has not been touched for a considerable period suddenly disappears when the assigned nurse's attention is distracted. Long sleeves of woolly jumpers, pockets of baggy trousers or jeans, and dustbins are common places where food is hidden or dumped.

CONTROL

Anorexics often feel that their lives are being controlled. Successful cheating—outwitting nurses, doctors, and parents—gives them a feeling of being in control of their own lives. It is always a sense of achievement for them.

Parents should be on the lookout when suddenly a daughter starts wearing baggy clothes. It is a ploy to conceal sudden and continuous weight loss.

The onset of the illness is indicative of a sudden change in eating habits.

What to look for:

1. Girls spend longer periods eating normal or small portions of food.
2. They start checking the number of calories in whatever they are about to eat.
3. They may cut their food in small pieces, which enables them to nibble.
4. They sometimes push their food to the edge of the plate. They watch as crumbs or large pieces fall over onto the mat or table.

5. Food, a vital sustenance for human beings meant to be enjoyed, becomes detestable.
6. Eating becomes a chore rather than an enjoyment. They will rather hide the food than to eat it.
7. Some will give excuses like "not feeling well" or "I have a tummy ache" to avoid eating or to be at the table with the rest of the family.
8. The bulimics may eat their food and suddenly excuse themselves from the family table. They return with signs or smells of vomit. The devious ones may use perfume to neutralize the smell of vomit.
9. Parents should plan and act in unison: any disharmony is exploited to the full.
10. Parents should try and be a step ahead all the time.

Early-detection, treatment programmes incorporating cognitive-behaviour therapy (CBT), counselling, and old-fashioned psychotherapy have improved over the years. Food is important, but any psychological problems have to be resolved as well.

Glossy images in magazines of slim fashion models are unhelpful.

Factors that are attributed to the condition known as "eating disorders" include parental pressure, family problems, unhealthy sibling rivalry, and emotional and sexual abuse; however, anorexia nervosa remains a complex illness.

Experience over the years and general opinion among professionals remind us that for even a hint of recovery to emerge at all in the treatment of an anorexic patient, all interested parties should be singing from the same hymn book. There should be no changes, no variations at all, in the interpretation and implementation of care plans. A new development or important information from any of the interested parties (such as parents or community workers) will point to a reappraisal of the care plan. Once the plan has been altered or sometimes totally changed in the case of the new important development or information, everybody should be informed. Fairness and firmness are the key factors.

STEADFAST

Initially, if an anorexic patient refuses to cooperate or denies being ill, that should not cause an immediate concern. What is important is for all interested parties to be steadfast. Whether the anorexic lacks insight into her illness, refuses to cooperate, or proves to be a difficult patient, she will soon comply with the treatment programme if all parties remain firm. The multidisciplinary team of consultants, doctors, nurses, dieticians, and therapists may find her a difficult patient because of her denial, lack of insight into her illness, or her sheer bloody-mindedness in refusal of treatment.

The community team comprising of the general practitioner, social worker, and key worker may be frustrated by the patient's lateness to appointments or failure to follow treatment programmes. Parents and family members may have difficulty keeping control or persuading the anorexic patient that she needs to engage with all the various disciplines in order to get well.

It stands to reason that when the anorexic does not cooperate with all the professional groups, there is one group that she will embrace and hope will keep her in their fold. Unquestionably, this group is made up of friends and acquaintances made before being taken ill and going into hospital. It is easy to conclude that the weakest group in these categories of interested parties are friends and acquaintances. They may not like to upset the patient by being frank—"You do not look well, you need to cooperate with the professionals." On the other hand, they could just be disinterested.

WEEKEND LEAVE AT HOME

Family members are the next group that the anorexic may try to manipulate in her bid to disengage or remain unwell. Parental love often becomes an impediment. Parents, especially some mothers, may claim that their daughters actually complied with an agreed diet plan during a particular weekend leave home. Sometimes, the anorexics dictate their own terms in the house, eliminating some mothers from their supervisory roles. The mothers do not, therefore, know whether the right amount of food has been eaten or indeed whether any food was eaten at all. In the presence of nurses, it is difficult for some mothers to betray their daughters. They reluctantly report that the diet plan was followed. Embarrassingly, the truth always comes out during the next-morning weighing session after weekend leave or after some days leave at home. A majority of anorexic patients returning to hospital from leave at home register a loss of weight during the following morning's weighing session.

It must also be stated that some anorexics go on leave and shut themselves away in their rooms from everybody, even parents and other family members. They refuse to cooperate with their pressured parents and return to hospital without following agreed-treatment programmes for the home leave.

MARY JO

Four weeks into Mary Jo's third admission into hospital for anorexia nervosa, the twenty-year-old was allowed home for some days leave. She soon found out that the community team rigidly insisted on enforcing the treatment programme prescribed by the hospital's multidisciplinary team. Her parents, from past experience, were not prepared to give her the benefit of the doubt, as they often had during her previous relapse.

Mary Jo's last hope was solace from her friends. She was surprised to find that on this occasion, they were not ready to feed her anorexic behaviour. They were frank with her and told her to get well properly before they would receive her in their midst. She returned to hospital in shock but had gained a considerable measure of insight into her illness. Mary Jo's attitude to structured-treatment programmes changed. She stopped pushing boundaries and particularly stopped arguing with dieticians and nurses over the number of calories and portions of food.

Progress began and she regularly earned weekend leave home. She was eventually discharged, but afterwards cooperated with her parents at home and maintained her regular appointments with the community team. She resumed her place at arts college.

Finally, she was back into the fold of friends whose support was positive.

"I thought that everybody was conspiring against me. My parents, especially my mum, who routinely used to give in to my demands, had changed during my third admission. She appeared heartless to me then," Mary Jo revealed to a therapist a week after her discharge.

She continued, "As for the community team, I never liked them anyway; especially the social worker who I thought was envious about my slim body. I would therefore walk out of appointments or not turn up at all at the slightest hint of grief from her."

Having spent some moments in a pensive mood, she made a wry smile and continued recounting her experience that dislodged her from her anorexic mode.

"My friends—my friends—they were all I had left after my perceived rejection by my parents and the frustrations I suffered in the hands of some members of the community team.

"When they put their shutters out," she paused, gave another wry smile, and resumed, "I thought it was the ultimate betrayal. Only there were no silver coins anywhere to be seen. Now, I know my parents and the community team did me a world of good. On reflection, I was finding it extremely difficult to get out of that anorexic stranglehold."

"So, how do you intend to fill your time profitably now that you have been discharged after a third admission in hospital?" the therapist enquired.

Mary Jo replied with enthusiasm, "I will keep all my appointments with the community team, hang out with my good friends, and in October return to college and complete my arts course. I will focus more than ever this time. Lest I forget, I will be very good friends again with Mum and as we were in the past. We'll, go shopping and spend Dad's money."

She then broke out in fits of laughter.

Unable to suppress her delight at Mary Jo's commitment and how revealing the session had been, the therapist giggled and concluded, "Good for you and the best of luck."

THE YOKE, FETTERS, AND THE COMPLEXITIES OF ANOREXIA NERVOSA

PAULINE AND BABY JEWELL

Pauline K. Paul at forty-two years old had spent almost half of her life in and out of hospitals with anorexia nervosa. She was first diagnosed with the illness at the age of twenty. She claimed that she was constantly bullied at school "for being fat". She somehow managed and concentrated on her studies and performed creditably well in her A-level examinations. She never thought of slimming to stave off the snide remarks and the blatant bullying by her peers.

During the first year at university, Pauline found it really difficult to cope. She found out that she was "the biggest girl" among the girls in the first year. It was disconcerting for her to see all the young male undergraduates around "the slim and sexy girls". Even more gallingly, the young men appeared not to notice her presence. Hitherto, Pauline had deliberately avoided any meaningful relationship with boys in order to concentrate on her studies. However, in the first year of university, she felt that she was mature enough to form relationships with boys and still cope with her studies. It was therefore a shock to her to be ignored, not because of her academic capabilities but because of her figure.

Consequently, she fell for the first male outside academic life who showed interest in her. She had baby Jewell at the beginning of the second year of university and hence had to stop her studies. She loved her baby girl dearly but regretted squandering her first opportunity at her quest for higher-academic laurels.

When Pauline was twenty-three years old with a two-year old baby daughter, she planned to resume her university education. She first embarked on a drastic slimming regime, which resulted in a massive loss of weight in a few months before the start of the academic year.

"This is the slim and sexy me," she said to herself as she did a twirl in front of her human-size mirror.

She was determined to show off her "slim and sexy body" to her former peers who were in their final year. More importantly, she was "ready to take on" any student, in the second and final years, who she felt was slimmer than she. She was so engrossed in this rivalry and competition that her studies suffered again, and she had to drop out of university. Her weight had plummeted from 56kg during the first year to 34kg with a low body mass index.

The first hospital admission happened at the age of twenty three. Her mother immediately took over the care of baby Jewell. Her partner had already left them. She had some periods away from hospital admissions; however, the pressure to compete and be "as slim as the slimmest girl or even better" utterly thwarted her maternal instincts towards her daughter Jewell. She lost partners—some prospective husbands—in rapid succession. The yoke of anorexia had not only put Pauline's academic aspirations in the doldrums but had mercilessly eroded any trace of her maternal instincts.

JUSTINA AND BABY BASSIE

Like Pauline, Justina was diagnosed with anorexia nervosa at age twenty three. She also had a two-year old daughter, called Bassie. Justina managed with the support of a well-organized community team and an understanding and supportive partner to minimize the number of hospital admissions over nineteen years. She could not, however, shake off the fetters of anorexia nervosa. Unlike Pauline, Justina had her partner, not her mother, to look after her daughter.

Bassie loved her mother so much that she would cry inconsolably whenever her mother was admitted into hospital. Bassie, at the age of twelve, started restricting her meals during the periods her mother was in hospital. The symptoms of anorexia nervosa were pronounced by the age of fourteen. This severely disrupted her secondary education. She would either vomit or use laxatives "to get rid of" any food she had eaten. Justina felt extremely guilty, but the fetters of anorexia impeded her from devoting her full attention in caring for her beloved Bassie. Thankfully, the community team worked wonders in keeping

Bassie away from hospital admission.

Justina, at forty two, compared to Pauline, managed better. However, with a twenty-one-year-old daughter who also restricted her food intake, competition and rivalry between mother and daughter drove her long-suffering partner to distraction. The women shopped together and stood in front of the mirror to declare who fitted better "in this sexy little dress".

COMPETITION AND
RIVALRY IN AN EATING DISORDER UNIT

Competition and rivalry amongst patients in an eating disorder unit is rife. Nevertheless, there is also a bond between some of them, which is at times as intense as the rivalry. Sometimes it defies explanation. I have seen many a seasoned professional shake his or her head in disbelief.

Cloe came to the aid of the multidisciplinary team when members were racking their brains to find out why her friend Maggie had suddenly become lethargic with blurred eyes.

They were anxiously awaiting the results of a blood test when Cleo revealed to the dietician in private, "Maggie told me that she had taken loads of paracetamol because she was fed up with 'being pumped up with shit' all the time."

Maggie was therefore rushed to the local accident and emergency. It was a timely intervention, which endeared Cleo to Maggie's relatives and all members of staff.

Maggie was admitted to the General Hospital for two days as a precautionary measure. During these two days, Cleo was very anxious for her friend to recover and return to the unit.

CLOSE OBSERVATION

Maggie, indeed, returned to the eating disorder unit and, as a precaution on the part of the multidisciplinary team, was put on close observation: meaning she was assigned a nurse who had to be with her all the time. In psychiatry, anybody on close observation always has the full attention of the members of the multidisciplinary team. When the observed patient is considered well enough—no longer a danger to herself and, indeed, others—the assigned nurse will be withdrawn. Close observation may take a few days or even weeks.

Meanwhile, the longer Maggie remained on close observation, seemingly enjoying all the attention, the more frustrated Cleo became.

She could no longer stand it and confided in a mutual friend, "Since Maggie came back from hospital, everybody is fussing over her."

Cleo, who had been making steady progress after a protracted period of effort from the multidisciplinary team, suddenly refused to comply with her treatment programme—no meals, no medication. On the third day of Maggie's return to the ward, Cleo cut herself on the arm, losing some blood. The consultant had no choice but to place her also on close observation. Yes! She had gained parity with her "friend" Maggie. Game on; let the competition begin.

Competition, rivalry, denial, deceit, manipulation, obsession, passion, paranoia, love, hatred, foolhardiness, irrationality, betrayal, suspicion, and lack of insight are just some of the traits of the sufferer of anorexia nervosa. The complexity of the illness sometimes baffles seasoned professionals with impeccable pedigrees.

BOYS? NOT BOYS! YES BOYS!!

GIRL POWER

Officially, a few years ago, anorexia nervosa was associated only with females. Not anymore. Now, we have boys or young, adult males being admitted for anorexia nervosa. Mind you, the last few years have also brought in their wake "ladettes"—girls drinking heavily into the early hours, totally "losing the plot" and falling about on pavements in town centres. Generally, behaviour that, until a few years ago, was solely associated with boys and young-adult males. During the same period, the emergence of girl gangs, some of them more vicious than their male counterparts, has compounded the problem for the general public. Some of these girls appear not to have had placid rosy-cheeks dolls to play with in their infancy, but rather Rambo-model machine guns as toys.

Moral crusaders of yesteryear, such as Mary Whitehouse in the 1970s, are quaking in their graves with disturbances of near-tsunami proportions. The current school of moral standard bearers and watchdogs (pardon the expression), I hasten to stress, do not know what has hit them. Some, I believe, are fervently praying that what has beset mankind is just a nightmare. They should wake up from their slumber and realize that it is for real.

ANOREXIA NERVOSA AND BOYS

"What is the world coming to?" an elderly gentleman once said, only for a precocious but recalcitrant girl to retort, "You haven't seen nothing yet."

The emergence of ladettes and girl gangs has shaken the adage "boys will be boys" to its foundation. In years gone by, the saying "boys will be boys" was an indication of resignation on the part of parents, school authorities, and the general public when the behaviour of boys baffled them or kept them at their wits' end.

Strides have been made by professionals in the last twenty years in the treatment of the illness. However, as already indicated, the general consensus is that it is complex The admission by these professionals, coupled with the phenomenon of boys suffering from this illness, emphatically blows away the myth that some girls become anorexic because they want to be like models. Admittedly, pictures of young and emaciated-looking models and some so-called celebrities do not help (as shown in the poem "Olivia asks for less"). Since emaciated male models are rare, why are boys and young adult males falling victim to the girl illness, anorexia nervosa? Arguably the influence of female models is minor, but it appears that there is a deeper underlying problem.

During my years in the NHS and since the early 1980s in the private sector, I had never cared for a male anorexic until about five years ago. Since then, the total number I have actually nursed or known about in another unit is fewer than ten.

POLITE AND COOPERATIVE

I have always got on well with male anorexic patients. They are polite and cooperative—in short, model patients, the type of patients overworked nurses in an intense environment always yearn for. It is no surprise that female nurses mother these male anorexics from the day of admission to the day they are discharged. As if that is not enough, they get an extremely favourable reception from the female anorexics. (Lucky chaps they have both groups at their beck and call.) Thankfully, of those I have had the chance with other nurses to care for none has had a relapse, as far as we know.

In comparison with the male anorexic, the female anorexic is a diva. This is borne out of my careful and unbiased observation over the years. What resonates in the objective analysis, conversation, idle talk, or tittle tattle of professional female nurses is that the illness makes many female anorexics manipulative, fussy (fastidious}, and wearingly demanding.

It appears less difficult for any male in general psychiatry to be confident of caring for young and male anorexics. On the other hand, liking food and being kind or religious is not enough. Experience and understanding remain crucial, as with the female anorexics. Official figures indicate that 1 in 2,000 men suffers from anorexia; while 1 in 200 women suffers from the illness.

Saying the wrong word to a recovering anorexic could unravel all the good work done by the professionals over a considerable period. Saying "well done" to anybody after they achieve something is customary in any language or culture. However, in the world of many anorexic patients, to be praised for consuming even a small portion of any meal accentuates a feeling of failure. After all, the illness makes the unfortunate victim eat as little as possible or, in the very serious cases, eat nothing at all if left on their own. Therefore, to eat something and be praised is an abomination to their way of thinking.

UNDERSTANDING IS CRUCIAL

One can understand an anorexic patient without necessarily agreeing with her.

1. Somebody has restricted her food intake to 300 calories (equivalent to 200ml of a fortsip drink) a day for a long time. Suddenly, in hospital this amount is doubled, which is still meagre for a daily intake. It is therefore perfectly logical that after a week or so on this double portion, the patient would "feel fat" or cry out, "I am fat." This is where the understanding is necessary. However, the next hurdle is to notify the patient that calories will be increased gradually to achieve targets until a healthy weight is stabilised with a maintenance diet. The average daily calorie intake for a twenty-five-year-old female is 2,000: for a male, 2,500; for a thirty-year-old female, 1,800; for a male, 2,000 calories. These figures should increase with a higher level of activity.

2. A visitor to an eating disorder unit told a patient that, when he saw her, he thought she was a member of staff. For a patient in a ward of unwell female adults to be told that she appeared like a nurse should, in a normal interpretation of the circumstance, be considered a favourable comment. The patient, instead of accepting the comment as a

compliment, became upset and shut herself in her room and refused meals and all attempts to open a dialogue with her.

When she finally came out, she told a friend that being referred to as a nurse meant she was fat. She needed a lot of reassurance to dissuade her from the thinking that she was "as fat as the nurses". She eventually stopped crying but was determined to eat as little as possible of the day's dinner and nothing of the pudding at all. On this account, nobody, not even the consultant, could persuade her to eat in order to maintain her slow but marginally encouraging progress. The result was a significant drop in her weight during the following morning's weigh-in.

This is a classic example of how the illness distorts the thinking of otherwise intelligent and rational young women.

BODY IMAGE PROBLEMS

Meanwhile, when the episode was recounted during the nurses' handover, Nurse Brown suddenly stood up looking a bit nervous. In my limited experience in the field of nonverbal communication, the expression on her face could be interpreted as, "Who is the cheeky little so-and-so calling fat?" Lo and behold, she rang the restaurant and cancelled her pudding for the day in favour of an apple. Nurse Brown then stretched the hem of her skirt all around as if to add a couple of inches to hide something—just like what the young adult females do these days. They leave home fully aware that their mini/micro skirts are two miles too short. Once in public, they start stretching the hems to create out-of-the-blue two more inches. The more they stretch, the more the skirts retract.

My Auntie Maureen moans as soon as she sees any of "these skirts [that are] are too short to cover anything".

She will pause and then conclude, "They might as well come out of their houses in the nude. Then we'd know where they stand with us." According to Auntie Maureen, "You'd think they will learn their lesson after the public display and exposure. The following day, they are back in public going through their routine."

Auntie Maureen is almost ninety years old. Age, if anything, has hardened her attitude to the "despicable behaviour of young people of today". She abhors every incident as if she has seen it for the first time: And she has been at it since the 1960s. There is no sign that she is slowing down. Do not even think about it. She does not need an optical aid to spot "a fashion disaster" a hundred metres away.

NARRATIVES AND REFLECTIONS

1. A twenty-year-old university student whose studies have been disrupted by the illness.

BROKEN HEART

I grew up in our neighbourhood with a boy of my own age called Peter. My parents knew his parents very well. We were very close from a very young age. In our teenage years, we studied together by spending time in the library or in each other's house. We went camping together and enjoyed the occasional holidays with members of both families. I had some girlfriends in our neighbourhood and at school. However, it seemed I enjoyed Peter's company more. He admitted feeling the same away, preferring me to his male friends. It was all very innocent.

Peter chose and sought employment in the financial sector after sixth form. I always wanted to test myself academically. In fact, I was the only member of my family from either paternal or maternal side to qualify for a university place. I wanted to finish university and eventually be a psychologist or a high-profile researcher.

I was about to go to university when both Peter and I realized that we were attracted to each other. He did not want me to go, admitting that it was selfish on his part. Hearing that from him appeared to awaken my own feelings, which I think I had subconsciously suppressed. On the evening of my departure to university, I was awake all night thinking about him. I think I managed to get only a couple of hours' sleep. I woke up in the morning and realized that my pillow was wet with my tears. They were tears of not being able to allow what had been kindled in me to start its emotional, romantic course. The feeling uncovered in me was very strong; however, my determination to excel academically and set a standard for other siblings and my future children was equally strong, if not marginally more potent.

FIRST YEAR AT UNIVERSITY

The first year at university was the best time in my life. I had a very supportive family, a soul mate waiting for me, and I was on course to achieving my academic aspirations. I could not ask for more. I was on top of the world.

I returned home after a very successful first year. I, however, found out that Peter did not respond to my calls and visits as usual. I did my best to stifle all intrusive thoughts of another girl stealing my childhood sweetheart from me.

A chance meeting with a mutual neighbour at the local supermarket laid bare my fears. She was a friend of Peter's sister, Lisa. She revealed that Peter told her that he had got another attractive girlfriend who was much slimmer. It was a shattering blow that left me feverish, cold, and above all deflated. I had not had any body-image problems before then. The last straw was mastering some courage to go to our local cinema. There, at a favourite spot, was Peter and a pretty-looking blonde.

I managed to see them before the lights went off. He pretended as if he did not see me. Under the pretext of going to the ladies, I left the cinema and went home.

SECLUSION AND WEIGHT LOSS

I spent the rest of the long summer holidays indoors venturing out only when necessary. I appeared to have lost my appetite and suddenly started losing some weight. I realized then that by restricting my diet I would appear slim and might win back my boyfriend. Initially, I felt that I could control everything. On reflection, denying myself the necessary daily sustenance became habitual.

My mum was the first to detect a change in my eating habits. I, however, denied everything and attributed my weight loss to academic pressure.

I started wearing baggy clothes to stave off those inquisitive stares from my mum. My dad appeared oblivious of the change in me. If he did, he kept his own counsel. I sometimes wondered whether my mum had discussed it with him. My twelve-year-old sister and ten-year-old brother appeared none the wiser. On the odd occasion I came out of my room, they played happily around me.

It was not until the first semester of my second year at university that my parents realized how much weight I had lost. I felt very weak and could not concentrate on my studies. I returned home twice in a month.

This is my first admission in hospital. I am doing my best to put the past behind me, regain my health, and return to university determined once again to realize my academic aspirations.

On reflection, I should have been mentally stronger and accepted the person I was. I had and still have something in my favour—intellect. I should have also confided in my mother, a trusted auntie, or anybody I trusted who would give me good counsel.

2. **A sixteen-year-old boy in hospital with anorexia nervosa, unable to take his GCSE.**

COPYCAT

I suppose one could say that in a family the children sometimes copy their parents' habits, good and bad. They sometimes follow the same professions. If some children do not copy their parents, they find older siblings the perfect role models. Girls may try and wear the same style of clothes and footwear that their older sisters wear. The hairstyle is also copied to the last strand.

Well, I am a boy so I could not wear similar style of clothes or copy the same hairstyle. My first recollection of my senior sister's illness was when I was ten-years-old. Marie is four years older than I. My parents, especially my mother, would spend a long time trying to get her to eat a simple meal. Sometimes our parents did not agree as to how to approach Marie. They often gave in to whatever she wanted—sometimes expensive presents.

When Marie was first admitted into an eating-disorder unit, the whole family was devastated. My parents attended family-therapy sessions with the consultant of the ward. I was included in only one of them. Each time Marie was discharged, it seemed my parents bought her even more expensive presents. She had her room beautifully decorated. Sometimes, I would be taken to our grandma's house so that my parents would be away for hours visiting my sister.

LOSS OF WEIGHT

It is difficult to say that I started copying my sister's eating habits. However, my parents soon realized that as Marie was beginning to recover from her illness, I had started restricting my food and losing weight. I started to get attention from my parents and seemed to like it. I did not get that attention when Marie was at home. The more attention I had, the more resolved I was to restrict my meals. I feigned illness and was absent from school for several days at a time. I was preparing for my GCSE but could not concentrate. Our dad blamed our mum who cried a lot, often feeling sorry for herself. One day my mum and I returned from a short trip to the shops and found a note written by dad. He blamed everything on mum and vowed not to return. He appeared caring enough to me, but maybe he could not cope anymore. Mum cried uncontrollably.

Grandma stayed with us for a few days and appeared to blame mum for the breakup of the family. Anyway with grandma in the house, I had all the attention I could get; Marie was still in hospital. We did receive the odd phone call from dad, who did not reveal his whereabouts. It appeared he had a partner. It was hard for mum to accept. She would not be consoled. Grandma did her best to support her and boost her confidence. It appeared to work when Marie recovered well and was finally discharged with a long-term care plan in the community. She had spent almost three years in and out of hospital.

A week after Marie's discharge, I was admitted into hospital at the age of sixteen years for anorexia. In the preadmission assessment the consultant concluded that the pressure of my pending exams and the illness meant I had to be admitted. Poor mum, it seemed "the nightmare", as she referred to it, had started again. I suppose for my future and my poor mum's sake I will do my best, get well, and return to my education. Marie is doing well now. She is attending art college. I am determined not to stay in hospital as long as she.

3. **An Old Anorexic**

I am forty-four years old. I have had this illness for twenty-eight years. I was first admitted at the age of sixteen. You could call me "an old anorexic".

I was bullied constantly at school for being fat. They called me all sorts of wicked names. I often returned home from school, went straight to my room, and cried for hours. I could not tell my parents or my school teachers for fear of being labelled a wimp or cry baby. I did not have any friends at school. I suppose there were a few girls who wanted to be friends but were afraid of the bullies.

The main bullies were not particularly bright. I suppose they were envious because during the first few weeks in our new form I was described by our teacher as being very bright. The bullying affected my confidence. My concentration suffered, affecting my studies. I finished sixth form with an average set of grades. My ambition of going to university and pursuing a career in medicine became just an empty dream.

LOW-GRADE JOBS

I first got an office job. However, the reoccurrence of this illness meant no job lasted very long and there were several breaks in what appeared to be good careers and prospective jobs disappeared. I have lost count of the number of admissions I have had and the number of consultants I have seen. I cannot rule out future admissions. However, I always use the community services very well to my advantage. I do not miss or skip appointments. I always give enough notice if I cannot attend any appointment, and I always make sure another is scheduled. I am always determined to stay discharged longer than the previous period spent away from inpatient admission.

On reflection, at least I should have told my parents or somebody in authority when the bullying was getting too much to bear alone.

4. INJUSTICE

False allegation ends over twenty years of dedicated work

I know anorexia affects young people, but it can affect for the first time an older woman like me. I am in my early sixties, a nurse by profession. I am qualified in three other professions. I have worked as a teacher, a branch manager with City Petroleum-Shell UK Oil, a cash-office manager for two different London boroughs, an income officer, and a public relations officer. I am currently on the books of one of the London boroughs as a presiding officer. I am always called during elections. I have officiated in all elections—general, local, European, and mayoral elections—for almost twenty-five years.

In addition to all that, I have worked over more than twenty years in nursing with a well-known private hospital. A twenty-four-hour rota system was introduced some months ago. I could not change from my permanent night contract and conform to the demands of the new rota system. I therefore changed into bank nursing after working for over twenty years with an unblemished record. As a bank nurse belonging to a pool of nurses, one is called upon to work when needed but has no permanent contract.

FALSE ACCUSATION

A new manager took over our unit. She blatantly refused to book me to work despite giving other RMNs shifts. She lied by saying that the shifts would be shared fairly. She also stated that I might not get any shifts at all when the permanent day staff came on night duty. I had been working on night duty continuously for years. It took seven agonising weeks before she revealed in a meeting I requested, the reason for excluding me from working. She unashamedly stated in the presence of a senior manager that she was told by another nurse that I refused to escort a patient out of the hospital after a twelve-hour spell on night duty. She also claimed that I left the ward with only one nurse in charge. Sadly, this incident never occurred. It was a fabrication on the part of the manager.

The unfortunate thing was that the new manager did not know me personally. She was inexperienced, unprofessional, uncultured, and unscrupulous. When she first met me just over two months after the alleged incident, she failed to enquire about the truth. She continued to exclude me from working for three months. In fact, after three weeks, I had decided not to work in that unit anymore and communicated my decision in a letter.

I did not get even the minimum help from key personnel despite several letters; one in particular written in the early hours. Having suffered hours of insomnia I went downstairs and, in a letter, pleaded my innocence. It took about two weeks before somebody responded. This response was prompted by a phone call I made stressing the atrocious treatment I was getting from a hospital I had served loyally for over twenty years.

Senior management allowed the new manager to use her position and savagely attack me, despite the fact that the Nurses and Midwifery Council rules stipulate, as I understand it, that a minimum of seven hours should elapse after a night shift before one can work again. In the same hospital, other nurses and I were forbidden in the last year to work on nights and return for a shift at 2:00 p.m. Even that was a break of six hours. How could any human being therefore justify compelling or asking a night nurse to continue after a long spell on night duty? My livelihood was snatched in an instant after over twenty years. I thought nursing was a caring profession.

Having been beset by all the above, I lost weight rapidly; hence, my admission in this hospital. On reflection by denying or restricting my food, I was punishing myself unnecessarily over a false accusation. I should have continued fighting my persecutors.

OTHER THOUGHTS AND OBSERVATIONS

There is always a battle going on in the mind of the anorexic. Deciding whether to eat (positive) or not to eat (timid or negative) is always at the forefront of their thinking.

In the home situation, experience shows that the negative attitude prevails most of the time. Anorexia is such a pernicious illness that parents, loved ones, caregivers, and anybody dealing with sufferers should always be firm and fair. Sometimes painful and difficult decisions have to be made. The sufferer will do her best to rebel or renege on an agreed plan. When she sees that the parent or the caregiver is steadfast and consistent, she will grudgingly comply, but she will surely try again at the next opportunity.

FAMILY TIES

Most of the time, it is difficult for a family member to follow rigidly a structured-care plan and to make any positive difference to the lives of anorexics. Professional intervention is needed most of the time.

Imagine a typical Monday morning in any household. Dad has to go to work; mum has to get little Johnny to the nursery on time to give herself an outsider's chance of not repeating the previous week's excuse for being late to a sceptical-looking Mr Grimsdale, her manager.

OUR MARY

Glued to the chair at the far end of the dining table is our Mary. She is oblivious of the commotion going on around her. She is looking intently (wickedly, I must say) at mum in order to get her parent to accede to reducing her already small portion of cornflakes, or she sits with her palm supporting a pale cheek. She appears disinterested in the current domestic proceedings.

Mum is changing little Johnny's top for the second time after a spill of Ribena. Dad is waiting impatiently and nervously. He needs to clinch that contract at the meeting scheduled for 09.00 hours in order to secure that elusive promotion.

What can a mother do? Well, nearly ten times out of ten she will give in and allow our Mary to eat the much reduced cereal. If our Mary happens to be bulimic, a quick, unnoticed dash to the toilet would result in the handful of cornflakes being offloaded into the toilet. Mum will then join everybody in the car and be at the mercy of what the rest of the new day brings.

Our Mary will go to school satisfied (Miss Timid or Miss Negative firmly in charge). Little Johnny will get to the nursery all right.

Dad does not look grumpy or nervous anymore. He is on course to clinch that contract. The minutes are ticking by, and mum is not at all hopeful of avoiding that sceptical look on old Grimsdale's face.

This morning's scene in the household of an anorexic is repeated every school day. The weekend beckons to usher in the two days of respite for mum from seeing Mr Grimsdale.

LYNCHPIN

In a majority of households, it is the mother who deals with the anorexic daughter and tries to carry on as normal as possible her role within the family. It is an understatement to say that it is difficult to cope with an anorexic patient. The anxiety, frustration, heartache, soul-searching, denial, and the guilt remain. The price that the majority of women pay for being mothers is incalculable. However, their worth is invaluable and irreplaceable in the family unit.

HOSPITAL ADMISSION

A professional setting in the form of hospital reduces the disparity between the negative and positive thinking of the anorexic. In hospital, structured and effective programmes administered by professionals who are not relatives offer a better chance of success. However, it is not all plain sailing. In hospital, the eating disorder patient meets other sufferers from whom she learns new tricks to avoid or restrict food intake. Sometimes, previous ideas are reinforced in hospital. In the domestic setting, the problem is that it is easier for siblings (especially sisters) to copy the anorexic's behaviour. It is also more difficult for parents or loved ones to ensure that structured care plans are strictly followed. It is always important that fairness and firmness are maintained irrespective of where the patient is receiving care.

KEY PARTICIPANT

The anorexic patient should be consulted and be involved (when well enough) in all plans or programmes for her care. Any care plan or programme structured for patients without their knowledge or input is likely to end in fiasco.

Once a care plan is drawn up and agreed on, the caregiver or the nurse should piously stick to it. Plans can be appraised, amended, or changed altogether if found to be ineffective. An innocuous request like "let me sit down for another two minutes" should, in most cases, be granted. However, care should be taken so that two minutes do not become sixty minutes. The anorexic patient will always push boundaries or constantly test the resolve of nurses, key workers, or parents.

The problem is whether in the home or in hospital, the patient has all the time in the world. It is the nurses who must worry about giving medication, writing notes, and other related duties. In some cases, because of the shortage of staff, the nurse becomes like our Mary's mother. She has to give in somehow, and what appears as an effective programme for the benefit of the patient becomes woefully diluted. Miss Timid has another feather in her cap.

RIVALRY

Rivalry among anorexic patients in an eating-disorder ward is another problem with which nurses have to contend. During meal times, the girls would be as hawkish as Dickie Bird on a sticky wicket. Food portions should be exactly the same for everybody. Not a grain, particle, or a crumb more or less. If a nurse has to reduce what appeared to be more than a generous portion from the kitchen, she has to be very, very careful. If she takes too much, the rest would be up in arms—"You are favouring her." This is a classic example of the illogical aspect of this illness. The patients are admitted as individuals to be treated, but each seems keenly interested in what happens to others. The patient perceived to be favoured would be ostracized until the next meal time, when another would be chosen to pick on. The thinnest patient would either be admired or become a rival.

SOLIDARITY

Solidarity among anorexic patients could go on for a long time until one of them breaks ranks and divulges a secret. It offers nurses one of the few chances to get a look into the inner life of the patients. It should be stated, however, that if a fellow anorexic is at serious risk, information will be passed from a member of the clique to save the situation.

EXERCISE

Some anorexics resort to excessive exercise to keep their weight low or avoid, in their thinking, being fat. Exercise in an eating-disorder unit comes in various forms. There is a very energetic one that keeps the floor shaking and alarms the staff. Then, there is the wriggling of the body and jerking of the legs under the beds clothes. Our Mary was an expert in this type. Throw in the thick duva, and even a hawkish nurse could not detect any movement.

"May I go for walk?" is an innocuous request in any situation or language but not in an eating-disorder unit. Health Care Assistant Miss Jones rued the moment she allowed our Mary out for a walk without seeking approval from a senior nurse. The girl secretly stayed out in the garden for thirty minutes and lost half a kilogramme of weight the following morning. These patients always look out for the novice staff or the new recruit.

Then, there is the very subtle, regular, and continuous movement of the leg in open view. Warn them one second, and they are at it the next.

WHO IS FAT?

Anorexics usually refer to themselves as being fat. They seldom call anybody else fat. Probably, they would not say anything to a genuinely fat person for fear of being exposed. One Monday morning, having finished giving medication, I got into an argument with our Mary. She would not drink even 10 ml of water with her paracetamol for fear of being "fat". We were standing in the corridor when Miss Jones, the new healthcare assistant approached.

Instinctively, we both stepped back to either side of the width of the corridor to allow her to pass. It was glaringly obvious that Miss Jones was a bit on the heavy side (if I may put it that way)—or may I say that she laboured as she walked. Momentarily, the argument ceased, and silence fell on both of us. Would our Mary stand side by side with Miss Jones and refer to herself as being "fat?" *Nah!* No contest.

Having seen the back of Miss Jones, our Mary resumed, "Why should I drink water and get fat when the tablet will dissolve in my stomach anyway?"

Our Mary was academically brilliant and an intelligent teenager with whom one could engage rationally on many topics as long as it was not about food or calories and, I hasten to add, tablets and "fattening" water.

It was occasions like this when non-professionals became baffled and speechless. A professional would understand but not necessarily agree. It was that occasion that made me remember my old headmaster at junior school, Mr Mensah. If he could not get a couple of known inattentive pupils to understand "a simple arithmetic problem" for the umpteenth time, he would retire to his chair, raise his hands to the heavens, glasses falling, and plead passionately, "Dear Lord Jesus Christ of Nazareth, come down and look upon your children."

He would then hold his head in both hands for some moments before trying yet again.

Thankfully, we do not need divine intervention these days to dislodge the entrenched views of the anorexic and pave the way for a full recovery. The multidisciplinary teams of doctors, nurses, dieticians, therapists, and cooks are already blessed with skills to help this vulnerable group. The success rate is now very encouraging.

WHO IS WATCHING WHOM?

Nurses pride themselves of being very vigilant, but patients watch nurses even more intently in order to exploit the slightest lapse. Patients exercising secretly are always on the lookout or listening for footsteps. They are quick in taking a position on the bed to fool the unsuspecting nurse.

I once told an anorexic that we had "seen it all." I told her that the two lady colleagues and I had about 100 years nursing experience behind us. She gave a wry and cheeky smile. My interpretation of it was "You watch me." She then broke into fits of laughter as she returned to the lounge.

I then thought to myself, *"You are only eighteen years old. You do not even know who Mrs Thatcher is."*

Academically, the majority of anorexics I had the privilege to engage with were brilliant. A considerable number were very creative. It stands to reason that if anorexics are reasonably well and a topic (away from food) is of interest to them, they become very rational in their thinking.

FATHERS

I always keep a special eye on fathers accompanying their wives to visit their daughters. Some fathers are very good and cope very well. Others appear nervous and unsure of what to do or say in the presence of their daughters. When other siblings are around, the fathers turn their attention to them while the mothers see to their anorexic daughters. Some fathers appear totally out of place.

I always say to myself, *"At least they have made the effort to come."*

A PLAN FOR RECOVERY

IN HOSPITAL

Nobody can fight anorexia except the victim herself or himself. I believe that professionals should seek out the person behind the mask of the illness. Once the personality prevails, recovery ensues.

The multidisciplinary team of consultants, psychologists, nurses, dieticians, and therapists.

1. A treatment programme formulated by this team is to be carefully implemented by all members of staff.
2. A programme that does not yield the expected results is reappraised and agreed changes made known to all concerned.
3. Occasionally, the whole plan is replaced by a newly formulated one. Sometimes a plan needs to be relaxed just momentarily to reward somebody who is genuinely doing her best but struggling to cope.
4. There are reasons why entire programmes have to be changed. The various hurdles to achieving an agreed target may, during implementation, prove unrealistically difficult, and therefore, the eventual goal becomes unachievable.

Conversely, an entire programme or plan could be considered ineffective after a period of implementation. A new presentation or important pieces of information not reported initially in the patient's case history will compel the leading consultant and other professionals to formulate another plan that takes into account the new facts.

5. Once a plan is working effectively, with the multidisciplinary team receiving the cooperation of all interested parties, a measure of success should emerge. This, then, forms the basis of the long, frustrating, arduous, and at times unpredictable road to recovery.

6. The more insight a patient has about her illness, the stronger the foundation for recovery.

AT HOME

1. Community teams are always informed by the multidisciplinary team in the responsible hospital about an impending discharge of patients. During the final CPA (Care Plan Approach) meeting, the decisions are taken to ensure effective continuation of care. A community team made up of a social worker and a key worker, with backing from the general practitioner, gets the cooperation and support of the parents. The members of the hospital multidisciplinary team are always available to offer professional expertise, should the need arise.

2. The parents' important role is to ensure that the discharged patient attends all appointments with the community team. If the discharged patient is continuing with her

education, in apprenticeship, or returning to work, the parents' support and their active encouragement remain crucial. In the absence of education or work, hobbies and other interests should be encouraged. The discharged anorexic patient should always be occupied to minimize or eliminate the daily preoccupation with calories, food, and body image. Positive distractions are work, voluntary work, studies, hobbies, and leisure.

3. All interested parties should play their roles effectively. When that is assured, the success, which the multidisciplinary team worked tirelessly to achieve, will be enhanced.

4. The diet plan and, where applicable, the prescribed medication regimen should be adhered to. Noncompliance and the possible drop in weight should alert the parents, the community team, and friends. Weight should be monitored closely.

5. Readmission should be arranged between the community team and the hospital consultant for a "top up" to stave off serious deterioration in weight. It is easier to stabilize the weight at a certain level, then improve it, than allowing a deeper drop before readmission.

AT HOME—NO PROFESSIONAL SUPPORT.

It is extremely difficult for parents and family members to care for anybody in the throes of developing the illness of anorexia nervosa or a discharged patient. The service provided in hospital with the community follow-up may not be perfect but it is extremely important. Professional engagement should be sought as a matter of urgency in either case.

WHO WANTS TO BE IN HOSPITAL?

Nobody wants to be in hospital and certainly not the anorexic patients, many of whom believe there is nothing wrong with them. Whenever I get the opportunity, I impress on them the importance of benefiting from the time spent in hospital where professional help is available.

I am always at pains to tell them, "While you are in hospital, your contemporaries are forging ahead with their lives in education, a chosen profession, work, engaging hobbies, or simply having fun as young people should, until adult responsibilities beckon".

I always ponder over the factors in the makeup of the illness that makes patients who are, for example, victims of bullying, sexual abuse, parental pressure, sibling rivalry, examination pressure, and broken romance use food as a cover for their illness.

Sufferers of the generation gone by used food as a cover. The current generation as already indicated are doing the same. No doubt, the next generation—unless anorexia is eliminated—will also use food as a scapegoat.

Anorexics in different countries, different cultures, different races, and different social backgrounds have all used food as a cover for their illness.

The challenge, therefore, is for all professionals in this specialist field to uncover the factor in the illness that compels sufferers to restrict their food intake or even starve themselves to death. Indeed, it is common knowledge that sustenance is vital for the maintenance of a healthy mental and physical state. A sustained period, therefore, of denying the human body nourishment is extremely dangerous. Could genetics and family, social, and cultural factors be attributed to this illness?

A breakthrough will be a pivotal piece in this jigsaw puzzle of an illness.

When the anorexia nervosa appears to have been unmasked for a meaningful period, these young adults and young women listen and ponder their future, including their academic and professional aspirations. It is always a delight to engage them in conversation. They are intelligent, rational, and at times witty and funny. During such occasions, the contents of the conversation are far removed from calories, food, weight loss, weight gain, laxatives, induced vomiting, excessive exercising, and blatant denial. What a refreshing change!

I am still working with anorexic patients. All professionals should always be hopeful, otherwise it would be unproductive to work in this caring profession. It is a part of the humanity we have in all of us as fellow human beings to keep up with the challenge posed by the uncertainties and complexities of anorexia nervosa.

SOME FACTS AND FIGURES

Since 2008, a total of ninety-eight children between the ages of five and seven have been admitted into eating-disorder units.

In the same period, ninety-nine children ages eight to nine have been admitted suffering from anorexia.

Between the ages of ten and twelve, there have been four hundred sufferers, and between thirteen and fifteen, the number stands at fifteen hundred sufferers.

These disturbing facts were released by the NHS Trusts under the Freedom of Information Act.

Research underscores the fact that anorexia has the highest mortality rate of any psychiatric disorder from medical complications linked with the illness as well as suicide. Twenty percent of anorexic sufferers die prematurely from the illness.

Grim statistics, but where there is a will there is always a way.

FOOD HAS CERTAINLY NOTHING TO DO WITH IT. IT IS THE ONLY INNOCENT PARTY IN THIS AFFAIR.

The Before and After

Lightning Source UK Ltd.
Milton Keynes UK
UKOW050000171211

183944UK00003B/1/P